Little
Pebble™

Habitats

All About
Grasslands

by Christina Mia Gardeski

CAPSTONE PRESS
a capstone imprint

Little Pebble is published by Capstone Press,
1710 Roe Crest Drive, North Mankato, Minnesota 56003
www.mycapstone.com

Library of Congress Cataloging-in-Publication Data
Names: Gardeski, Christina Mia, author.
Title: All about grasslands / by Christina Mia Gardeski.
Description: North Mankato, Minnesota : Capstone Press, [2018] | Series:
    Little pebble. Habitats | Audience: Ages 4–8.
Identifiers: LCCN 2017031566 (print) | LCCN 2017039448 (ebook) |
    ISBN 9781515797708 (eBook PDF) | ISBN 9781515797586 (hardcover) |
    ISBN 9781515797623 (paperback)
Subjects: LCSH: Grassland ecology—Juvenile literature. | Grassland
    animals—Juvenile literature.
Classification: LCC QL115.3 (ebook) | LCC QL115.3 .G37 2018 (print) |
    DDC 577.4—dc23
LC record available at https://lccn.loc.gov/2017031566

Editorial Credits
Marissa Kirkman, editor; Juliette Peters (cover) and Charmaine Whitman (interior), designers;
Eric Gohl, media researcher; Katy LaVigne, production specialist

Photo Credits
Shutterstock: AlinaMD, 7, BGSmith, 11, David Whitemyer, 5, dibrova, back cover, interior (grassland
illustration), Dmussman, 20, Jeeri, cover, Oleksandr Fediuk, 19, Papa Bravo, 17 (top), Pedro Helder Pinheiro,
17 (bottom), pornpoj, 15, Ricardo Reitmeyer, 1, Robert L Kothenbeutel, 10, SnelsonStock, 6, tomtsya, 9,
Volodymyr Burdiak, 13, Zeljko Radojko, 21

Table of Contents

What Are Grasslands?

Grasslands are lands
of grass.
Animals live in the grass.
It is a busy habitat.

The Prairie

A prairie is flat.

It is hot in summer.

It is cold in winter.

winter

Deer eat the grass.

This makes it short.

Few trees grow.

Prairie dogs dig.

Hawks spy.

hawk

prairie dogs

The Savanna

A savanna has hills.

It is warm all year.

The grass is tall.

Elephants graze.

Zebras run.

Lions hunt.

Fire!

A fire burns the grass.

The roots do not burn.

Rain falls.

Grass grows.

Grassland animals grow too.

Glossary

deer—an animal with hooves that runs fast and eats plants

graze—to eat grass

habitat—the home of a plant or animal

hawk—a large bird with sharp claws and a strong beak that hunts small animals

prairie—a grassland with hot summers and cold winters

prairie dog—a small animal that digs and lives in tunnels in the prairie

savanna—a grassland that is warm all year

zebra—a grassland animal with hooves and stripes that runs fast

Read More

Arnold, Quinn M. *Grasslands.* Seedlings. Mankato, Minn.: Creative Education, 2017.

Knight, M.J. *Grasslands.* Fast Track: Who Lives Here? Tucson, Ariz.: Brown Bear Books, 2017.

Polinsky, Paige V. *Protecting Grassland Animals.* Awesome Animals in Their Habitats. Minneapolis: Abdo Publishing, 2017.

Internet Sites

Use FactHound to find Internet sites related to this book.

Visit www.facthound.com

Just type in 9781515797586 and go.

Check out projects, games and lots more at
www.capstonekids.com

Index